YOU'RE MAKING THIS. WAY TOO HARD

ANGELO VALENTI, Ph.D.

You're Making This Way Too Hard

Find YOUR easy way to NJOYLFE

© Copyright 2023 Angelo Valenti

All rights reserved.

No parts of this publication may be reproduced, stored, or transmitted in any form or by any means, electronic, mechanical, photocopying, recording, or otherwise, with the prior written permission of the copyright owner and publisher.

Cover and Interior Design by Dino Marino, dinomarinodesign.com

Print ISBN: 979-8-223-13492-3

YOU'RE MAKING THIS WAY TOO HARD

FIND YOUR EASY WAY TO NJOYLFE

ANGELO VALENTI, Ph.D.

SPECIAL INVITATION

Join the NJOYLFE Community

Message me on

1. LinkedIn:
   https://www.linkedin.com/in/angelovalentiphd/

2. Instagram@companypsychdoctor

3. Send me an email at: angelo@angelovalenti.com

4. Facebook@Angelo Valenti

Everyone on my email list will receive a free digital copy of my forthcoming *You're Making This Way Too Hard: Find Your PERSONAL Easy Way to NJOYLFE* workbook.

TABLE OF CONTENTS

*"None of us are getting out of here alive,
so please stop treating yourself like an
afterthought. Eat the delicious food.
Walk in the sunshine. Jump in the ocean.
Say the truth that you're carrying in your heart
like hidden treasure. Be silly. Be kind. Be
weird.
There's no time for anything else."*

~Nanea Hoffman

INTRODUCTION

Hi there! Thanks for picking up my book.

Maybe you did so because the license plate on the cover aroused your curiosity.

That's my actual license plate. I've had it since 1991. I created it right after my divorce (more on that later), and it's been on every car I've had since. I make a pretty good living as a consulting psychologist, and I'm a car guy, so NJOYLFE has been on several higher-end cars, mostly Mercedes.

About 10 years ago, I parked my Mercedes SL550 in the parking lot of a casual dining restaurant (I'm a car guy, not a food guy) and went in to pick up my take-out order.

It took about 10 minutes to put my order together, and when I got back to my car, I found a note on the windshield. It read, "I would enjoy life too if I had millions of dollars and drove a $110,000 Mercedes!" I know how this sounds so far.

You're thinking, *This asshole is just bragging because he makes a little money and drives nice cars.*

Bear with me because here's the point of the story. When I read that note, I wanted so much to talk to the person who wrote it and let them know that they had cause and effect backward.

I don't enjoy life BECAUSE I have whatever stuff I have. I have whatever stuff I have BECAUSE I enjoy life. I'll get back to "stuff" later, too. If you want to see the actual note, email me (angelo@angelovalenti.com), and I'll shoot you a picture.

Maybe you looked past the license plate and picked up the book because something in your life just isn't working. Welcome to the club! Everyone has issues, some big some small. Whatever issues you might have are the same issues people have been having for thousands of years.

I was having a conversation with my best friend, Tommy, and he said he thought there were more mental health issues now than in the past. I said no, but free-floating anxiety is not much of a problem when foraging for food. What's changed is that we are much better at identifying those issues and have developed better ways to help people with those issues. Most of us don't think the devil possesses people, are witches or are genetically inferior if they display symptoms of mental illness.

I will leave significant mental health issues to the professionals who have dedicated their careers to helping people with those. I'm going to focus on the problems we've created for ourselves. If you're stressed out at work, pissed at your spouse, envious of the rich and famous, feeling like you're a failure or a loser, addicted to something unhealthy to dull the psychological pain, or just vaguely miserable on a daily basis, I'm here to tell you it doesn't have to be that way.

Are you ready for the rah-rah, you can be whatever you want to be, spiel? *Ain't happening.*

Thousands of self-help and self-improvement books, courses, videos, and gurus exist. But how much have people really improved? Dale Carnegie published *How to Win Friends and Influence People* in 1936, and I don't think anyone has written one much better than that since then. Most self-help books are like cotton candy. They're delicious when you're reading them, and they give you a nice sugar high. But once the high wears off, you're right back where you started. Why is that? There is a ton of good advice in these books, so why does the sugar high wear off?

It's because people aren't willing to put in the actual work needed to change. Change is hard. It's especially hard when it's somebody else telling you what and how to change. Before they even read the book, people know in their hearts what they need to do, but they don't do it.

This isn't a self-improvement book. *This is a self-acceptance book.* The purpose isn't to show you how to be rich, famous, well-liked, thin, pretty, smart, or any other things you've been led to believe will make you happy.

I want to show you how to make life easier for yourself and, in doing so, find the contentment necessary to NJOYLFE.

Are you ready to explore?

CHAPTER ONE

YOU GOT THIS

Have you ever said to yourself, *"Life isn't fair"*? Well, you're right.

Do you want to know what fair is? Fair is where they have the Ferris wheel, the merry-go-round, cotton candy, corn dogs, and carnival games. There's no such thing as fair because what's fair for one person might be unfair to another. If someone says, "You know what would be fair?" you might as well bend over and grab your ankles because here it comes!

In theory, fairness is a worthwhile goal. However, that's another matter entirely in practice, although we still try. Watch a group of children playing some time. If they're playing a game, the first thing they do is agree on a set of rules. These rules are designed to allow both teams to have an opportunity to win without the deck being stacked against them. If we want to learn a new game, the first thing we need to know is what the rules are. Just as games have rules, society has developed a set of rules, called laws, designed to do the same thing, allowing everyone to "win" without being placed at an "unfair" disadvantage. Even with rules and laws in place, somebody wins and loses.

All of us have certain advantages and certain disadvantages. This combination of advantages and disadvantages is unique to each of us and allows us to be who we are and do what we do. However, we are bombarded daily with messages that encourage (brainwash) us into focusing on our disadvantages.

We're too tall, or we're too short. We're too fat or too thin. We're too black, white, old, or young. Further, we're too poor or rich, and on and on and on.

This steady stream creeps into our minds and leads us to believe we can't be what we want to be, do what we want to do, or have what we want to have because of our disadvantages. This creates discontent, divisiveness, and despair and can make life miserable.

MISERABLE IS NOT OUR NATURAL STATE. WE COME INTO THE WORLD WITH A SENSE OF JOY, WONDER, AND CURIOSITY. WE HAVE TO BE TAUGHT TO BE MISERABLE.

Fortunately, many people don't fall prey to this constant negative messaging. Instead of focusing on the limitations their disadvantages put on them, they focus on the opportunities their advantages provide them. They direct their minds and their energies toward what they can do, not what they can't do, who they are, not who they're not, and what they have, not what they don't have. These are the people who enjoy life.

As a teenager, I wanted to be a professional baseball player. I knew I was good at two things: school and sports. I became a good player, got some college scholarship offers, and was scouted by Major League teams. There was only one problem. I wasn't good enough. I gave it my all, but the ceiling of my baseball potential wasn't high enough.

That left me with the other thing I knew I was good at: school. I got into a good university, Case Western Reserve, got good grades, played football and baseball for the love of the game (no scholarships), and got a degree in psychology.

Do you know what that prepared me for?

Nothing except for more school, so I went to graduate school and got a Ph.D. in psychology. I tell you this because it's an example of me focusing on my advantage (academics) rather than my disadvantage (not good enough at baseball).

Happy people use their advantages to their benefit and don't let their disadvantages define them.

You can do the same. You're terrific just the way you are, and there is a ton of joy waiting for you out there. You just have to believe it. In the following chapters, we're going on a journey to find your easy way to NJOYLFE.

CHAPTER TWO

THERE ARE SYSTEMS ALL AROUND YOU

According to the *Merriam-Webster* Dictionary, a **system** is a group of interacting or interrelated elements that act according to a set of rules to form a unified whole.

The world is made up of a myriad of systems. Some of these systems are big: governmental systems, educational systems, communication systems, transportation systems, religious or spiritual systems, economic systems, financial systems, social systems, etc. These systems are so pervasive and ingrained that most of us don't spend too much time thinking about them unless something happens where they smack us in the face.

These extensive systems exist for a few reasons. They provide some sense of order and predictability (an illusion), they create standard operating procedures, and here's the biggie: they control almost every aspect of our daily lives. At various times, one of these systems will be controlling your life more than the others, but there's seldom a time when none of them controls you.

We are confronted with a few choices since we're all impacted by these systems.

First, we can choose to fight the system. There are many examples of people who have fought the system and achieved remarkable results. Think Socrates, Jesus, and Martin Luther King, Jr. Of course, they were all murdered for their efforts, but still.

Second, you can choose to change a broken system for the better. Think Abraham Lincoln and John F. Kennedy. Hey, wait a minute. They were murdered, too. Are you picking up on a trend here? *The system doesn't like when you mess with it.*

Third, you can ignore the system. Try not paying your taxes for a few years and see how that works out for you. I'm sure some lucky people are so completely off the grid that the system doesn't affect them. It must be working because I don't know who they are, so I can't name names.

Finally, you can find a way to work the system to your advantage. I don't mean gaming the system by cheating, lying, manipulating, or slithering through loopholes for personal gain. I mean learning how the system works, recognizing the rhythm and timing within that system, and finding ways to navigate the ins and outs in a way that allows you to NJOYLFE without the system repeatedly smacking you in the face.

Within each extensive system, there are lots of smaller systems. These are the systems that impact your life all day, every day. Family, friends, work, school, hobbies, clubs, recreational and entertainment activities, neighborhoods, and the city where you live are all systems with subsystems within them. Whenever one of these systems taps you on the shoulder and says, "Just so you know, I'm getting ready to mess with your life," remember your four choices. Fight, change, ignore, or work it.

MAKE THE SYSTEM WORK FOR YOU

The Selective Service System was conducting a lottery to determine who would be drafted to take an all-expense paid trip to Vietnam.

It was December 1, 1969, and I was sitting in the living room with all my fraternity brothers, watching the process unfold on a small black-and-white TV.

Ordinarily, it would have been almost impossible to get all of us in the same room at the same time for any reason, but this was different. I was a junior then and still had a year and a half left on my college deferment, so I didn't feel the same impending doom that my senior fraternity brothers felt.

The process began with numbers 1 through 366 being written on slips of paper and placed in opaque capsules. Those capsules were then placed in a big glass jar.

Then, the fun began.

The first capsule drawn read 258. The 258th day of the year is September 14th; that date was assigned the draft lottery number of one. The second number corresponded with April 24th, and so on, until all 366 numbers were called.

As a side note, in 1969, females weren't eligible for the draft, but they would be if they held a draft today. So, if you're a young adult feeling nervous, anxious, confused, or uncertain about what the future holds for you, try to imagine how we felt waiting to see if, literally, our number was up.

My lottery number was 191. It's not the kind of number you ever forget. From reading the newspaper and watching the network news, the only way to get current information (or misinformation), I knew that any numbers greater than 250 were safe and those less than 150 would probably get drafted. I was right there in the iffy zone. I called my local draft board and was told that in 1970, they would call numbers up to 225. Yikes! I still had my senior year to go, so that 225 number was stuck in the back of my mind.

I wanted to go to graduate school after I graduated, so I started applying to various programs at the beginning of my senior year. In the second semester of that year, I was accepted into several programs, including my first choice, the University of Georgia.

I called them to let them know I wanted to attend but had to wait until I knew my draft status. They understood and said I wasn't the only one in that predicament. The second semester rolled around, and I made another call to my draft board. This time, they told me that in 1971, they would only call up to 125.

Yippee! What a relief.

It was good because I don't think military life would have suited me. I probably would have tested into officer's candidate school, gone through that, and become a first lieutenant. Then I would have led a platoon (or whatever lieutenants lead) in Viet Nam. Once I arrived, there would have been an excellent chance that I would have been shot, either in the chest by the enemy or in the back by my own men. It happened more often than you might think.

In May 1971, my fiancée and I drove from Cleveland to Athens, Georgia, where I signed up for classes and looked for an apartment. We married in September and moved all our stuff (in a small trailer) to Athens.

I know this is a long intro, but you'll get the point soon.

I began classes in the Social Psychology department in September. The minute I arrived on campus, my goal was to get my Ph.D. as quickly as possible (I was shooting for four years), and I knew I would have to use all my talents to do so. When I met my classmates, I quickly realized that I was the dumbest person in our class. Not dumb in general (I did get into graduate school, after all), but dumb compared to my peers. I also realized I had way more street smarts than any of them. I'm an introvert, so I usually hang back and observe in a group setting. I noticed that my classmates liked to argue with the professors, I guessed, to show how smart they were. I also saw that the arguing did not go well for them.

That's where I figured out a significant feature within the system of the psychology department. *Professors do not like to be argued with.* I made it a point not to argue with professors, whether I agreed with them or not. While this didn't give me a chance to display my "brilliance," it did allow me to sail through my classes without extra assignments or heartburn. It was the easiest path to take, and it worked beautifully.

As cowboy wisdom says, *"Never pass up an opportunity to shut up."*

I soon figured out a second prominent feature within the system. The more time you spent in the building, the more likely you were to do or say something stupid. This would have interfered with my overriding goal, so I decided to stay away from the department unless I absolutely had to be there. For that, I earned the nickname "The Phantom," which was kinda funny. I wasn't insulted but instead took pride in it. Again, no extra assignments or run-ins with my professors.

The Ph.D. program at Georgia required the completion of two major research projects: a master's thesis and a dissertation. After two years of classwork, those two significant hurdles were menacingly staring at me. This was where observing the system and figuring out how to make it work for me paid off.

Georgia is a big-time university, and the professors are expected to do research and get that research published—the old "publish or perish." During my first two years, I became aware that one of my professors hadn't published anything in a while and was pretty stressed about it. I spotted an opportunity to get help with a research idea for my master's thesis.

I made an appointment to meet with this professor, Sam (not his real name). Sam was a great guy and the coolest professor in the social psych department. I mentioned that I was having difficulty developing a research project. Every time I started thinking about it, I freaked out, and the creative part of my brain froze up. I wondered if he had any ideas that might be worthy of study. He said that his wife was an attorney, and they had just talked about a new law that passed in Florida, allowing 6-person juries rather than the traditional 12 for non-capital cases.

Sam thought it might be interesting to see if 6-person juries reached different verdicts than 12-person juries. Social psychology covers group behavior, including group decision-making.

That sounded like fun, so off to the library I went (my only option in 1973). If you're getting bored with all this academic stuff, I'll skip the particulars and tell you that I conducted the study using college students as jury members.

There was a running joke among psychologists that psychology is defined as the systematic study of the behavior of the college sophomore and the white rat.

My study lent credence to that joke. Anyway, the study turned out great, and after a couple of months of writing, my thesis was accepted. Not only that, but Sam and I also had an article based on the study published in the premier social psychology journal. Since I had no idea how to write a journal article, Sam did most of the writing, but it was my research, so my name was listed first. I like to think that, in some small way, I saved Sam's ass.

Then, since my thesis and classwork were out of the way, I could concentrate on starting that pesky dissertation. Before I tried to come up with another research idea, I decided to see if the system would work again. One of the other professors, Jacob (also not his real name because both professors are still alive), was, to this day, the most intelligent person I've ever met. I mean brilliant! Unlike Sam, Jacob was a prolific researcher and had many articles published, so I knew the lure of another article wouldn't work on him. However, he was actively researching a theory he had developed, and I thought there might be an opening there.

I visited with him and asked if there were any aspects of his theory that he hadn't investigated yet. He mentioned a few areas, and one sounded particularly interesting, so I asked if he thought that area might make a good study for my dissertation. He said yes, and I was on my way. We devised a methodology to test the theory, and I was off to the library again to research the subject.

I conducted the study, again using college sophomores, who will do almost anything for extra credit.

The results were not as clear-cut as in my previous research, but Jacob was a statistics whiz and got positive results using a method I'd never heard of. To top it off, we got the research published in a journal (again!).

There were two more hurdles before I could start calling myself a doctor. The first was writing the dissertation, a time-consuming, soul-sucking ordeal before computers. The second hurdle was defending the dissertation before a committee composed of the professors in the department. I turned in my dissertation in the early summer of 1975 and started applying for college teaching jobs. I landed one at Oklahoma City University, so we moved to OKC in August. My dissertation defense was scheduled for October, so I returned to Athens to defend my work.

Naturally, Jacob was on the committee, and when the other committee members asked me a tricky question, Jacob chimed in and helped me answer it. After all, it was his theory, and he was emotionally and intellectually invested in it. I had left OKC as an ABD (all but dissertation) and returned as a newly minted Ph.D., and I did it in four years. None of my classmates came close to getting theirs in that timeframe. They fought the system, and I found a way to make it work for me.

One of the beautiful things about systems is that they resist change. What does that mean for you? *It means that once you figure out how a system operates and how to make it work for you, it works almost every time.*

Keep this in mind as we search for your easy way to NJOYLFE.

CHAPTER FOUR

TAKE THE CONTROLS

Hopefully, you're on a mission to find an easy way to enjoy life. However, before you can do that, you need to do some digging for WHY you're not enjoying life right now.

There are a lot of possible reasons (or excuses) for why you're stressed, angry, disappointed, frustrated, anxious, nervous, fearful, bored, resentful, envious, hung up on the past, or whatever else is keeping you from waking up every morning with a smile on your face and a song in your heart.

The shovel we will use to dig into the WHY is a psychological concept known as **locus of control.** (I do like to throw around my over-education occasionally.) Psychologist Julian Rotter introduced this concept in the 1950s. He referred to an individual's belief about how much control they have over their lives and how much they can influence the outcomes of events. Rotter stated that an individual's *locus of control* is either internal or external, which can significantly impact how a person views actions and events.

According to Rotter, people with an internal *locus of control* believe they have control over their behavior. As a result, they take responsibility for their behavior and the outcomes of that behavior. Also, they confidently approach challenges, tend to be healthier, and often experience greater career success. People with an external locus of control believe that events are determined by external factors such as luck or outside forces. These people tend to have a fatalistic attitude toward life because they don't think they have the power to change their lives. People don't have a 100% internal or external locus of control, but developing an internal locus of control is worthwhile if you want to find your easy way to enjoy life.

In life, you're either the puppeteer or the puppet. You're the puppet if you believe that forces outside of yourself are controlling your life. If you believe you control your life, you're the puppeteer.

Here's why locus of control is so important.

We are bombarded daily with images and stories in entertainment, the news, and social media that paint an idealistic picture of happiness. We measure our self-worth by how many likes we get on our posts, we see staged videos and think they're real, watch sports and entertainment stars jetting off to exotic locations, read stories about business moguls owning five houses around the world, we buy the *Sports Illustrated* swimsuit edition (for the articles, of course), and we follow social media influencers. (I can't even believe that's a real thing.)

This is designed to show us the system's concept of happiness and force us to realize that we don't measure up and never will.

How are we supposed to feel good about ourselves when everyone else supposedly has it much better than we do?

> **WE'RE WATCHING EVERYONE ELSE'S SCRIPTED, STAGED, AND EDITED HIGHLIGHT REEL WHILE AN EXAGGERATED BLOOPER REEL OF OUR LIFE IS RUNNING IN AN ENDLESS LOOP THROUGH OUR MINDS. THE SYSTEM WANTS US TO BELIEVE THAT IF WE CAN GET TO A POINT WHERE WE CAN LIVE THE ARTIFICIALLY PRESENTED LIVES THAT OTHERS ARE LIVING, WE'LL BE HAPPY.**

Falling into this trap is like playing the old arcade game Whack-a-Mole. Some of you younger folks might not have played it, but here's how it goes. You approach the game, which features a few holes in a board and a rubber mallet. When you put a token into the machine, little mole dolls pop up from the holes briefly and randomly. The goal is to hit as many moles as possible in the time allowed.

Envying someone else's success is like a mole popping up. Whack that one down, and the "they're more attractive than I am" mole pops up. Whack that one down, and the "my boss hates me" mole pops up. Whack that one, and the "that guy really pisses me off" mole pops up. It never ends. How do you win the Whack-a-Mole game inside your head?

DON'T PUT THE TOKEN IN THE MACHINE! The minute you put a token in that machine, you become the puppet.

I will ask you a few questions, and they're questions only YOU can answer.

Question 1: What gives you joy?

Not happiness—joy. Happiness is overrated. It's a transitory phenomenon.

Let me give you an example. Let's say you're a big football fan, and your favorite team is the Cleveland Browns. Having grown up in Cleveland and been a Browns fan all my life, you already have my deepest sympathies.

The Browns are playing their bitter rivals, the Pittsburgh Steelers. In the first quarter, the Browns go up by a touchdown. *You feel happy.*

Then the Steelers come back and take a 3-point lead midway through the second quarter. *You feel unhappy.*

The Browns run back the kickoff for a touchdown. *You feel happy.*

The Steelers storm out of halftime and take a 10-point lead going into the fourth quarter. *You're unhappy.*

The Browns stage a furious comeback to tie the game with 2 minutes left. *You're happy.*

The Steelers kick a field goal with 5 seconds left, and the Browns lose. *You're unhappy,* or more probably, miserable.

All of this for a football game. I've been there. Striving for happiness is just another case of you being the puppet because the system or others control so much of what makes you temporarily happy.

That being said, I'll use the words "happy" and "happiness" throughout the book, but please know that what I mean is "joy, contentment, and self-acceptance."

Joy is the feeling you have when everything seems right with the world. You can hardly wipe the smile off your face, and you find yourself breaking into song for no reason. Lots of things can bring you joy. The birth of a child, reading a good book, seeing a movie that moves you to laughter or tears, seeing someone you love do something special, accomplishing a meaningful goal, or achieving a personal best in an activity you enjoy.

I DON'T KNOW WHAT GIVES YOU JOY, BUT IF YOU DON'T, IT'S ESSENTIAL THAT YOU DISCOVER IT.

I should say rediscover because I'd be willing to bet you felt joy almost nonstop when you were a little kid. That's because when you're a little kid, simple things give you joy—climbing a tree, jumping in a puddle, playing with your favorite toy, petting a puppy, exploring a stream with friends, jumping off the high dive for the first time. Think about what gave you joy when you were a kid, and try remembering what that felt like because that's a significant step in your journey to NJOYLFE.

Question 2: What do you like about yourself?

I'd be willing to bet you haven't asked yourself this question lately, maybe never, yet it's important to answer it openly and honestly as your journey continues. From the time we're young, we're told we shouldn't brag about ourselves, that modesty is a virtue. If you boast or brag, people might call you an egomaniac, a narcissist, or, at the very least, someone suffering from "I" strain.

At the same time we're being taught not to brag about ourselves, we're also told that we need to be likable. Well, this is your chance to brag about yourself to yourself. Try to put aside the times that you have been criticized by others or told you're not good enough. If you hear that stuff enough, it's easy to internalize it and start believing it about yourself.

The undeniable fact is that you have many admirable qualities. These qualities contribute to your friendships, interactions with others, work performance, hobbies and interests, and the variety that is the tapestry of your life.

It's time to stop hiding yourself from yourself. Do you have a knack for making people laugh? Are you kind toward others? Are you competitive? Are you compassionate? Are you mechanically inclined? Are you good at math? I could go on listing questions all day. I don't know the answers to these questions or the others you could ask yourself, but YOU do.

Take stock of yourself. Let yourself feel good about all the parts that make up the whole of you. If you want to find your easy way to enjoy life, you must love yourself. *Self-love is not the same as selfishness.*

SELF-LOVE IS RECOGNIZING YOUR WORTH AND YOUR VALUE.

Remember the last time you took an airplane trip? When everyone has boarded, and the plane is ready to take off, the flight attendant makes a safety announcement. One of the announcements states that oxygen masks will drop if there is a sudden loss of cabin pressure. If that happens, you are supposed to pull down on the mask to release the flow of oxygen, and if you are traveling with a child or someone who needs assistance, you should *put on your mask first* before helping someone else.

The same applies to your life. You can't help others if you don't take care of yourself first. It's impossible to love others if you don't love yourself honestly, and if you don't love yourself, why would you expect others to love you? There's an old song: *You're nobody 'til somebody loves you.* I think that's bullshit. You're you in all your glory whether someone loves you or not. But if you love yourself, you'll find that people will be drawn to you like you wouldn't believe. If you love yourself, you don't need others to give you validation. Nobody cares about you as much as you care about you.

Here's a true story to give you an idea of what I mean. I love to play golf, and I play a lot of it. A few years ago, a friend and I were paired with another twosome at our club. I knew the other twosome but hadn't played golf with them before. On any golf course, there are several sets of tees from which you can play, depending on your age and skill level. These tees vary the overall length of the course. Since I was older than 65 at the time, I usually played the senior tees, which on the first hole were about 30 yards ahead of the regular men's tees. The other three players were younger than me, so they were playing the regular tees. I told them, "What the heck? I'll play the regular tees, too." One of the other guys asked, "Peer pressure?" I replied, "Nope. If you don't have any peers, you don't have any peer pressure." It was something I wanted to do, not something I felt I had to do.

One more true golf story (for now). When I joined my country club in 1986, I didn't know many members, so I often played a round by myself. On one such occasion, I was finishing the front nine when one of my clients drove by on his way to his next hole. He said, "Angelo, are you playing with all your friends?" I replied, "No, just my best friend." At times in my life, I wouldn't have been able to make that statement. I'll share that part of my journey later.

If you love yourself, it's easier to feel confident. We're all subject to self-doubt, but confidence and belief in yourself can overcome that self-doubt and allow you to take the actions that lead to achieving the goals you've set for yourself.

Confidence comes from measuring yourself based on what you think of yourself. It is the unshakable belief that you can make what you expect to happen through your abilities, talents, and effort. Confidence comes from continuing to try until you get better, not listening to the doubters, and, most importantly, maintaining a positive attitude. Competence breeds confidence, and a positive attitude keeps you going as you develop competence. True confidence, not self-aggrandizement, is contagious and magnetic.

Confidence isn't cockiness. Cocky people love to talk about all the great things they have and all the wonderful things they've done. I think cocky people are trying to convince themselves that they're worthy by selling others on their worthiness. In my experience, the more people talk about themselves, the less they're really saying.

If you love yourself, you're going to be more resilient. Resilient people can bounce back from adversity or setbacks. Children tend to be resilient because they face a lot of "firsts" and make many mistakes. However, they have an innate learning mindset and don't let those mistakes or setbacks keep them from building the skill sets they will need throughout their lives. A first step in building resilience is approaching a setback as a child would, as an opportunity to learn and grow. By focusing on the positive rather than the negative, you're more likely to push through that setback and be better prepared for future adversity that comes your way. It's hard to enjoy life if you let every bump in the road keep you down.

If you love yourself, remembering fond memories and smiling is easier. You can also look back on less pleasant memories and realize that you learned something from them, and they contributed to who you are today. You're less likely to feel resentful, angry, hurt, depressed, or victimized.

You can't go from not loving yourself to loving yourself by flipping a switch, but you can take those first steps right now. Here's how:

1. **Quit being so damned hard on yourself!** Perhaps you've been listening to others telling you why you don't measure up and won't amount to much. Maybe you've fallen into the trap (it's easy to do) of believing what the system has been telling you about what it means to be successful, attractive, and worthy.

   You haven't been getting these messages by accident.

They're designed to make you think you can't control your life and must depend on some outside force to make you "happy." This outside force is telling you that you should start talking nicely to yourself. It's not only OK to compliment yourself; it's what you should be doing. Be proud of yourself. Focus on the positives.

Henry Ford said, "Whether you think you can or think you can't, you're right."

Start thinking that you can and saying it to yourself often. Be like the Little Engine That Could ("I think I can, I think I can"). Turn a mistake into an opportunity to learn, a problem into a challenge, and disappointment into a growing pain. You can actually reprogram your brain by repeatedly saying positive things about yourself. You might say that sounds like you're believing your own bullshit, but when you start genuinely feeling better about yourself, it's not bullshit anymore; it's reality.

Let's say you cooked a great meal for some friends. They're impressed with your culinary abilities and lavish sincere praise on you. What would your first reaction be? If you haven't learned to love yourself, you might say, "I think I put in too much pepper," "The sauce was too runny," or another comment. Here's a much better response to praise. **Thank you.** That's it. If you want to say more than a simple thank you, say **it was my pleasure to cook for you.** You'll know what sounds better to you, but the point is to acknowledge that you did a good thing and did it well and that you appreciate that your friends recognized and enjoyed it.

2. **Get off your ass.** If you watch any TV at all, especially in the evenings, you'll see many commercials that fall into two categories. The first set of commercials will show people happily sweating away on their Pelotons or some other exercise machine, canoeing down a river, climbing a mountain, or running a 10K. The second set of commercials will be for medications for every type of disease or condition possible, most of which I've never heard of. These medications have a list of side effects that sometimes sound worse than the condition they're treating. If the possible side effects include anal bleeding, stroke, and death, I believe I'd learn to live with restless leg syndrome. Both sets of commercials make the same point: if you don't have your health, you don't have shit. They're not wrong. If you want to enjoy life, getting yourself in as good shape as possible is a good idea.

I realize that some physical conditions aren't under your control, but even if you're dealing with medical issues, there are things you can do to improve your health. The first thing you can do is be a little less sedentary. You don't have to run a marathon to improve your health, but if running gives you joy, have at it. Personally, I think running is great unless you compare it to not running. Remember, all the dead bodies on Mt. Everest were once highly motivated people, so maybe take it easy. How about taking a walk? Chances are that wherever you live, there is a nice walking trail nearby. I take a 2-mile walk in the woods almost every morning at a state park near my house. It's a great way to start the day and gets me in touch with the beauty of nature. It's hard to be in a lousy mood walking in the woods.

The second thing you can do is try to eat a little better. Food is one of the great joys for many people, and I'd be the last person to tell you not to enjoy a good meal. I'm talking about the crap that too many of us eat. You don't need to stop eating crap, just cut back a bit. Try a half bag of potato chips instead of a whole bag, eat ice cream three days a week instead of daily, and drive past McD's occasionally. If you've got a genuine eating disorder, please get professional help. There's no shame in admitting you need help.

The year was 1978. I was a psychology professor at Oklahoma City University, teaching an evening social psychology class. Before class one day, a very large man walked into the classroom. He was about 6'1" and weighed (as he soon told me) 400 pounds. He walked up to me and said something to this effect: "Hello, professor. I'm Tom. I'm returning to college after 20 years. I just went through my third divorce, I weigh 400 pounds, and I'm going to lose 200 pounds in one year." This got my attention, and I asked him how he planned to lose the weight. He said, "I'm going to eat two pieces of dry toast with coffee in the morning, a salad with low-calorie dressing and a Tab for lunch, and chicken or beef and a vegetable with another Tab for dinner. Also, I've joined a gym, and I'm going to work out every day." Some of you might not know what Tab is, but it was one of the first "diet" soft drinks. If you've never tried one, don't. *Tastes awful.* Mercifully, it's been off the market since 2020.

I'd put on a few pounds since college and decided to join Tom's gym and work out with him when possible. As the semester went on, I watched Tom work out like a madman, and I noticed that he seemed to have more of a spring in his step as he entered the classroom. I also noticed that I was losing a little weight and had more energy.

By the end of that semester, Tom had lost 50 pounds and looked noticeably thinner. I had gotten in the best shape since my college football days. Tom took a couple more classes with me, and I continued to see him at the gym over the next several months. At the end of his one-year goal, he actually lost 200 pounds. He had a lot of extra skin hanging on his frame, but he had surgery to remove it. He looked like a different person, and his attitude improved along with his appearance. Tom was a serial entrepreneur who opened a weight loss clinic to help others achieve their goals.

3. **Take a nap.** I know I just suggested that you get off your ass, but naps are a special case. They're right up there with massages when it comes to doing something nice for yourself. Napping is common in many cultures, but some people view napping as a luxury or a sign of laziness. I view it as a guilty pleasure, except without the guilt. Many of us fill our days up to the brim with a combination of work,

family, recreational, and social activities. If that describes you, do you find yourself exhausted, irritable, frustrated, or distracted by the end of the day? Your body and mind can only take so much. If we get tired during the day, we drink coffee or an energy drink to keep going. Let me tell you that a 20–30-minute nap can do wonders for you, both physically and mentally, especially if you can take that nap at around 2-3 p.m. when most of us naturally experience that post-lunch dip in energy. Science backs me up on this. There is ample research documenting the health benefits of napping. Besides all that research, naps just feel great.

4. **Do things you enjoy.** How many times have you said to yourself, "I should be. . ." followed by something on your mental to-do list or something someone else wants you to do but doesn't matter much? We all fall into this trap, letting others dictate what we should or should not do. You know damn well you'll finish your work in time if it's important enough. If it's not that important, maybe it's time to reexamine your career choice. We all have activities that we especially enjoy, and a big part of enjoying life is doing things that give you pleasure, satisfaction or put a smile on your face. Only you know what those activities are for YOU.

It's amazing how many varied activities or hobbies people are into. Our society has thousands of subcultures, one for every hobby, interest, or recreational activity. I have mixed feelings about social media, but in terms of finding people with similar interests and learning about things you enjoy, social media is hard to beat. Assuming they're not illegal or immoral, do whatever activities you enjoy with passion and enthusiasm and without worrying about what others think of you.

I love to smoke cigars, but only under two circumstances: when I'm awake and on days that end in Y. I especially love smoking cigars on the golf course. When I'm playing, I keep a cigar in my mouth, even when I'm swinging. Someone asked me once if I played better with a cigar in my mouth, and I replied, "I don't know. I never play without one in my mouth." Some people think it's a nasty habit, but fortunately, I don't care what those people think.

I interviewed a candidate a few years ago, and in my interviews, I always ask what a person likes to do in their free time. Most of the answers I get to this question are ordinary and almost predictable, but this candidate hit me with a new one. He said, "I collect animal tracks." I asked what he meant by that, and he told me, "I walk in the woods with a bucket of plaster and a trowel, and when I see an animal track that I haven't seen before, I make a cast of the track, take it home, and put it in my collection." For some reason, this struck me as wildly amusing, and I had difficulty keeping a straight face. But being the professional that I am, I stifled my laugh as best I could and asked him how many different animal tracks he had collected. He said, "Well over 100." I replied, "You mean to tell me that over 100 animals are running around the woods where you live?" He answered, "Oh, no. I've traveled all over the US and several countries to collect tracks." Well, duh, I thought. All I could say was, "Good for you and good hunting." Now, there was a guy doing what he enjoyed enthusiastically—a lesson for us all.

5. **Get real.** You might have grand ideas about what you'd like to be or do, and you might even be able to make it happen. The question is, do you have the motivation? There are more dreamers than doers in this world, and relatively few dreamers turn their dreams into reality. A dream without drive, persistence, the willingness to take risks, and single-mindedness is a fairy tale. Many of these dreams are again

based on what the system says we should be or do. Setting realistic, attainable, and meaningful goals is an easy way to enjoy life. The goal of reading 100 books a year can feel overwhelming. The goal of reading one book a month feels much more doable. Running a marathon can take months of training. Walking 2 miles a day is doable. Starting your own business can be terrifying. A side hustle is doable. Remember Tom's weight loss? That took tremendous self-discipline and perseverance. Losing 1 pound a month is doable. Before you set a goal, ask yourself WHY you want to achieve it.

If you don't have a good why, it probably won't happen. However, if you do have a good why, keep that why at the top of your mind. Write down the goal and the why. Visualize how you'll feel when you accomplish that goal. Tell someone close to you about your goal and ask them to encourage you (and gently nag you a little, if necessary). Publicly committing to a goal makes achieving that goal more likely. Take pride when you make progress, and REALLY take pride when you reach your goal.

6. **Associate with people who are enjoying life.** How you feel about yourself and life generally has much to do with whom you spend your

time. If you want to feel good about yourself and life, spend time with people who feel the same about themselves, make you laugh, think, and help you see all the good in and around you. There is a saying that misery loves company. That's wrong. *Misery loves miserable company.* People who feel miserable don't want to be around upbeat, positive people, and those upbeat people don't want to be around miserable people.

My wife Rachel and I were invited to dinner by a couple we recently met. We met them at a nice steak house, and almost from the minute we arrived, the complaining started from the other couple. The dining room was too crowded and dark, there was too much noise, the server was too slow, the food was not prepared properly, the wine was subpar, and the prices were too steep. When dinner was over and the checks were paid, the other couple said, "That was so much fun. We'll have to do it again sometime soon." Rachel and I gave each other subtle glances, and when we got to our car, I asked Rachel, "Did I miss the fun part of that dinner? All I heard was complaining." Rachel agreed, and we made sure we didn't go out with that couple again.

A great dinner with fun people can be a memorable experience, but an evening like our one with the complainers is a waste of time and a buzzkill. Sometimes, you must endure people you'd rather not be around, but when you have a choice, choose the people who add to your sense of joy.

Loving yourself and believing in your self-worth is a big step in finding your easy way to enjoy life. Be kind to yourself, practice self-care, rid yourself of the toxic people in your life, and most of all, do something that gives you joy every day.

CHAPTER FIVE

DEALER'S CHOICE
(and you're the dealer)

It's poker night. You and your friends have gotten together for an evening of cards, alcohol (probably), telling and retelling jokes and war stories (definitely), and trash-talking. The dealer decides which game the group will play, and the deal rotates. Maybe you're not very good at seven-card stud but are an ace (pun intended) at five-card draw. When it's your turn to deal, what game will you play? Five-card draw, of course. That's the right choice for you, even if it might not be the best choice for some players.

Who, what, and where you are today is the result of the choices you have made up to this point. If you're going to make choices, you will have to make judgments. Whenever I hear someone say they don't judge, I want to call "bullshit." If judging is bad, why is there an entire profession called JUDGE?

In our personal and professional lives, we make thousands of judgments daily, some big and some small. We judge what route gives us the best chance to get where we want that day. We judge what to wear, what to eat, who to spend time with, what to do, what to watch or listen to and whether we like it, what to believe, who to vote for, and, well, you get the idea. When judging people, we apply a different standard to ourselves and others. As Steven Covey wrote, "We judge ourselves by our intentions and others by their behavior." Unfortunately, for some people, intending to do something is the same as doing it. Judgment allows us to figure out what works and doesn't over time. If every possible choice carries an equal weight, we might as well flip a coin when faced with a decision. Mark Twain said, "Good judgment is the result of experience, and experience is the result of bad judgment."

You might not be too happy with who, what, and where you are or be thrilled. In either case, the vital thing to remember is that YOU made choices that have led you to this point. I realize that some people start their life's journey in much more difficult circumstances than others. You can't control where or when you were born, who your parents were, or what genetic combination gave you your biological characteristics. That's the hand you were dealt. However, how you played that hand was up to you.

When we look back on our lives, too often, we focus on mistakes, opportunities we've missed, people we've hurt or disappointed, and stupid things we've done. We've all done things that we wish we hadn't done. I know I have. While that's part of our story, consider it a chapter, not the whole book. Your past can either be your teacher or your jailer. The choice is yours.

I went to my 10-year high school reunion in 1977. The 10-year reunion is a weird one. If you went to a big high school like I did, it's the first time you've seen many of your classmates since graduation. You're still in your 20s, and your personal and professional journeys are still in their first steps. Some of your classmates are established in their jobs, some are married, some have children, some are still in school, and some are trying to find themselves.

I was painfully shy in high school. I had a group of close friends and a wonderful girlfriend (Ellen, God rest her soul). I was also the quarterback on the football team and the baseball team captain, so for that reason alone, more people knew me or of me than I did them. I was also clueless in high school about the social dynamics around me. Just how clueless I had been became evident at the reunion when I learned that several classmates had attended for the sole reason of confronting someone who had wronged them in some way in high school. These people had been carrying a grudge for 10 long years, while most of my classmates and I had only thought of high school when a song, an event, a movie, or something else jogged our memories.

> *"Holding a grudge is like drinking poison and waiting for the other person to die."*
>
> ~ Unknown

I wondered what it was like to hold on to such strongly negative feelings for so long. I also was sure that the person who did the "wronging" probably had long forgotten about the incident that caused the trauma. I'm not discounting how traumatic high school can be. I'm just saying that it's very personal, and the same event can elicit different reactions. Here's where choice comes in. You can choose to let it go, forgive, set your sights forward, and recognize your worth.

Rather than putting yourself in the jail of the past, try this instead. *Look back on all your great choices and decisions that allowed you to write an uplifting, exciting, fulfilling chapter to your book of life.* It's a fact that some of the decisions we make turn out great, and some don't. Most fall somewhere in between. If you want to make decisions that help you find your easy way to enjoy life, you first must believe that you can make those decisions, and the proof that you have that capacity is in the great decisions you've already made.

Here are some of the great decisions you can start making right now.

Just say no: Do you sometimes feel you have more to do than you have time to do it? Is every minute of the day filled with tasks, chores, or activities? If this describes your daily life, it's easy to feel overwhelmed. Sit down and think about how your days get so jam-packed. Are you doing things that are meaningful and important to you, or are you responding to requests from others? It's easy to lose control of your time without even realizing it. Time is the only commodity that we all have in an equal amount. The only difference is what we choose to do with that time. I know you want to be helpful and cooperative, but to gain control of your time, you need to be willing to say "no." In his post *Meditations on Strategies and Life, the blog by Ryan Holiday,* Holiday states, "You have to understand: Everything you say YES to in this life means saying NO to something else." If you say yes to working late, you say no to dinner with friends or family. If you say yes to binge-watching a series, you say no to reading or exercising. Saying "no" is a choice you must be willing to make, or your time will be at the mercy of others, and let me tell you that people will suck as much time from you as you're willing to allow. When someone asks you a yes-or-no question, there are two possible answers: YES and NO. No is a perfectly acceptable answer; it will make your life easier to enjoy in many ways. I must admit that when I started my consulting practice in the last millennium, I didn't say "no" much to clients or potential clients. I would say "yes" and then go back to my office and figure out how I would do what I said I could.

This is a common practice in business, especially among entrepreneurs, consultants, and salespeople. They want to build their brand and businesses and are reluctant to turn down opportunities. However, if you keep saying yes to everything that comes your way, you risk being over-committed, frustrated, and burned out.

SAYING NO LETS OTHERS KNOW YOUR BOUNDARIES AND KEEPS YOU OUT OF SITUATIONS YOU'D RATHER NOT BE IN.

You've been invited to a social event. There are some social events that you enjoy and look forward to, but this is one that you don't want to go to for a variety of reasons. You're worried you might disappoint the person who invited you, but you know there's a good chance you'll be miserable at the event and looking for an excuse to duck out early. You have a choice to make. Don't go and risk disappointing the inviter, or go and be kicking yourself the entire time. In that situation, I opt to stay home and not be miserable. Whoever invited me might miss me for a minute, but there will be so many other people there that I won't be missed for long. There aren't many parties that I'm the life of anyway. I know this is my introvert coming out, but even if you're an extrovert, ensure you're socializing for your reasons and not for someone else's.

You don't have to make excuses or give reasons when you say no. Be honest and direct. You don't owe anyone an explanation, but you can say, "I just don't have time for that," or "I can't commit to that." Some requests, like from your boss, family member, or friends, can be more challenging to say no to, but when you realize that "no" is an option, you'll be better able to prioritize which requests to say yes to and which to turn down. Saying "no" is a skill that gets easier with practice.

When you see how much time you've freed up to do things you enjoy, how your stress level has decreased because you're not trying to please everyone, and how much better you feel about yourself, you'll gain a genuine appreciation for the benefits of saying no.

Be grateful: If you're wondering what you have to be grateful for, the fact that you're alive to ask the question is an excellent place to start. Gratitude is an outlook on life or a mindset that focuses on being thankful for the good things in your life, big and small.

Gratitude could be as simple as appreciating a beautiful sunset, the smell of a flower, a child's laugh, or your dog excitedly wagging its tail when you come home.

You can develop a habit of gratitude, and once you do, you'll find opportunities to feel grateful everywhere you turn. Maybe you've heard the phrase "attitude of gratitude." It might sound trite, but it has power.

Here are some things you can do to improve your sense of gratitude:

1. Start a gratitude journal: Write down three things you're thankful for each day, no matter how small you think they are.

2. Say thank you.

3. Do something nice for someone else.

4. View situations with an optimistic eye.

5. Show and feel empathy towards others.

Be polite: An older man (probably about my age) was walking up the stairs of a large office building with glass doors. He saw a reflection in the glass of a young woman walking a few steps behind him. When he reached the door, he held it open for the woman. She looked at him indignantly and said, "You don't have to open the door for me because I'm a woman." He replied, "I didn't open the door for you because you're a woman. I opened the door for you because I'm a gentleman." This might sound old-fashioned, but politeness never goes out of style.

The great philosopher Vin Diesel said, "Being a male is a matter of birth. Being a man is a matter of age. But being a gentleman is a matter of choice." Politeness means showing respect, kindness, and consideration toward others, which goes a long way in building your reputation. I don't think people value their reputations as much as they once did, but they should because their reputation strongly influences how the world sees and reacts to them.

While it seems evident that we should be polite toward others, the sad fact is that many people aren't. Every day, we see in the media stories about people committing violence against others over seemingly trivial matters, airline passengers getting tossed off planes for angry or rude outbursts, thieves breaking into stores and stealing valuable merchandise, customers and employees being uncivil toward one another, and businesses putting profits before people. Oh, and don't get me started about social media. People say things to others on social media that they wouldn't dare say face to face, and they can often hide behind anonymity. It appears that the consequences for being impolite or discourteous just aren't there. You can even become famous if you're discourteous in a particularly clever or attention-grabbing way.

Want to be more polite? Say please and thank you. I've come across something lately that irritates me.

I'm at a restaurant and have just had a great dining experience. The server hands me the check, and I say, "Thank you. I really enjoyed the meal and your service." The server replies, "No problem." When did "no problem" become a response to "thank you?" To me, it sounds like there could have been a problem or that a potential problem existed, but in this particular case, the problem didn't happen. When I mention this to people, I get one of two reactions. Some people say, "That gets on my last nerve too," while others say, "Quit being such an old fart" or "It's a generational thing." Metaphorical flatulence notwithstanding, I still think "you're welcome" or "it's my pleasure" are better responses than "no problem."

Being polite means respecting others' time. Tardiness or, worse, not showing up at all sends a clear message that you think your time is more valuable than the other person's. You never have to make an excuse for being early. If something makes you late, there are many easy ways to let the other person know. If you don't even do that, don't be surprised if you're not taken seriously or dismissed altogether. I've heard more than one executive say, "If you're early, you're on time. If you're on time, you're late. If you're late, you're out."

Take a deep breath and reflect on what you will say or do and how it might impact others. It's okay to have an unexpressed thought, although many people seem unaware of that, especially on social media.

Don't argue with idiots: You're scrolling through your social media of choice and see a post that says butter pecan ice cream is the best. You happen to think that mint chocolate chip is the best ice cream. The post goes on to cite studies that show all the great things about butter pecan, including graphs and other statistics. Mark Twain wrote, "There are three kinds of lies: lies, damned lies, and statistics." You comment on the post with your statistics, touting all the great things about mint chocolate chip. Then, the comments start coming in. The butter pecan people rip the mint chocolate chip people, and vice versa. You think the butter pecan people are idiots, and the butter pecan people think you're an idiot.

This back and forth can go on for a while, but if you notice, *nobody changes their opinion, so what have you really accomplished?*

It's like sitting in a rocking chair. It occupies your time but doesn't get you anywhere. You've wasted your time, raised your blood pressure, and achieved nothing besides finding that some people agree with you and others don't. Didn't you know that already?

I used ice cream as a trivial example on purpose, but the same applies to any disagreement on social media. Whether it be politics, sports, religion, entertainment, science, economics, or any of the other myriad topics that lend themselves to strong opinions one way or the other, posting on social media is not going to change anyone's mind. It's no different than arguing about views in person. If you want a lively discussion, fine, but realize you won't come away with a victory.

Arguing with idiots is like telling someone to calm down. One of my favorite comics was *Calvin and Hobbes* by Bill Watterson. In one of his comics, Hobbes, a stuffed tiger, says, "NEVER in the history of calming down has anyone calmed down by being told to calm down." The system is designed to keep people arguing with one another. This keeps everyone from thinking about issues in a reasoned and unemotional way. There is a possibility that the other side might be correct, but once the arguing starts, the analysis stops.

However, the short anonymous talking points don't lend themselves to study.

I know it can be hard to resist, but what are the alternatives to arguing? First, you can scroll past the butter pecan post. Second, you can comment with "Bless your heart." Here in the South, "bless your heart" can indicate genuine sympathy, but more often, it means "you're a complete idiot" in the most condescending way possible. It's the first cousin of "With all due respect" and "No offense, but," which are almost always followed by something disrespectful and offensive. Third, you can comment with, "You're certainly entitled to your opinion." No more, no less. Fourth, you can close your social media, go to the freezer, scoop out some mint chocolate chip ice cream, and savor it, believing in your heart (and stomach) that you're right. This is truly the easy way to enjoy life.

CHAPTER SIX

CAN YOU RELATE?

"The only consistent feature of all of your dissatisfying relationships is *you.*"

This nugget of sarcastic wisdom comes from the website Despair.com. It's a great site with many parodies of the motivational posters you see everywhere in offices. While most of their parodies are clearly meant to be sarcastic and funny, this particular one has more than a bit of truth baked in. Have you ever used the old break-up line "It's not you, it's me"? Well, chances are it **is** you.

If your choices broadly define who, what, and where you are in your life, your relationships define the quality and richness of your life. Your family, your romantic relationships, your friendships, your work relationships, and your broader circle of acquaintances play a significant role in how much you enjoy your journey through life. Some of these relationships are long-lasting, and some are more fleeting, but they all influence you.

I got married in 1971. I was 22 years old, fresh out of college, and on my way to graduate school. I was also wholly naïve, immature, insecure, and unprepared for the ups and downs of a long-term relationship. My wife, Sue, was a very nice young woman dedicated to building our life together. We had two great children together. We were married for 20 years. The problem was me. I had no idea who I was, what I wanted, where I was headed, or how to behave to get there. I was clever enough to fake it through interactions with others, including Sue. But I was living a lie: all style, no substance. I was trying to be all things to all people, and, as a result, I wasn't being anything to anybody. We got divorced in 1991. It was clearly me, not her.

The idea of a marital bond between two people dates back to the ancient Greeks and Romans. In those days, you were lucky if you lived past 30. If the wars didn't get you, the disgusting living conditions and rampant diseases would. Poor nutrition and hygiene were prevalent. Childbirth was no picnic either, for the mother or the child. If you got married at 15 and were likely to be dead at 30, that's one thing. If you get married at 22 and have a good chance of living into your late 70s, that's something else altogether. When you hear two people say, "We drifted apart," it's easy to see how that can happen.

My failed marriage caused me to take stock of myself. I realized I wasn't the person others thought I was or the person I wanted to be. So, I decided that I would either learn from my failures and grow as a person, or I wouldn't inflict myself on anyone else. I did some serious soul-searching and recognized what I needed to do to improve my value to myself and whomever I wanted a relationship with. Over time, I became what I think was and is an improved version of myself. I believe that people reinvent themselves every 7-10 years, and those reinventions change the course of their journey.

Besides my two wonderful sons, something unexpectedly great came out of my failed first attempt at being a husband. I met my second wife, Ginger, when we were both separated from our first spouses. Ginger was beautiful, smart, funny, and charming. She also had a 2-year-old son. Some of my friends cautioned against dating someone with a small child, but I had already raised two boys and knew how much I enjoyed doing so. It didn't take long before I was smitten. We dated for a while, and it became apparent that things were getting serious. One evening, I handed Ginger a sheet of legal paper. She asked what it was, and I told her, "This is everything I can think of that's wrong with me. Some of this comes courtesy of Sue, and some comes from me, but I agree with almost all of it, so if we're going to be together, you need to know that this is what you're getting yourself into." She read the list, smiled some, laughed some, and shook her head some. Then she told me she thought she could live with the list.

Ginger and I got married in 1995. We bought a house together and began our married life. A few months later, I came home from work and had the following conversation with Ginger:

Ginger: The light switch in the guest bathroom is out. Will you fix it?

Me: No.

Ginger: What do you mean, no?

Me: I mean, no. It's on the list.

Ginger: What list?

Me: The list I gave you when we were dating. Number seven says, "I don't do home repair or improvement projects."

Ginger: I thought you were kidding.

Me: Nope. Let's call an electrician. They need to make a living, too.

Ginger was an extrovert: fiery, emotional, expressive, and funny. She wasn't the life of the party;

she brought the party with her. I'm an introvert, reserved, introspective, unexpressive, but also funny. A great example of "opposites attract." When we met, her friends didn't think we fit together, but after we'd been together awhile, they saw the connection. We had a great marriage. In 2009, Ginger was diagnosed with ALS, a degenerative disease that ravages the body but leaves the mind intact. She fought it for three years but passed away in 2012. Without going into detail, I learned much about myself, others, and life through that experience. If I wasn't convinced that you should cherish every day before Ginger died, *I was undoubtedly convinced afterward.*

I met my wonderful wife, Rachel, in 2013. I wasn't sure I wanted to be in another relationship, but there was an instant connection. I felt it, and so did she. We dated for three years and got married in 2016. Rachel is also an introvert. Our idea of a great party is one we're not invited to. We are an example of "birds of a feather flock together." Don't put too much stock in proverbs. I didn't make a revised list of everything wrong with me, but I told her about it and explained that I probably wouldn't change much at that point in my life. I believe we've discovered the secret to healthy and fulfilling personal, professional, and recreational relationships. *Want to know what it is?*

Quirks! That's it. Quirks are those little idiosyncrasies that make us unique. Quirks can be habits like chewing on ice or jingling your keys, unusual behaviors like not allowing the different foods on your plate to touch or snorting when you laugh, phobias like a fear of water or bugs, or tells like pulling your ear or rubbing your nose when you're nervous. A funny thing about quirks is that to the person who has the quirk, the quirk doesn't seem that quirky, but to the people they encounter, it can be a defining characteristic. My list is an example of quirks spelled out directly. Watch *Monk* if you want to see an example of quirks with the volume turned up. Most people's quirks aren't as extreme as his, but everyone has them. We have that one friend who's always late, the coworker who insists on telling you a joke when you're trying to concentrate, the sibling who points out the silly things you did as a kid, the grandparent who wraps all the furniture in the house in plastic. The list of quirks is almost endless because much of the quirkiness lies in the eyes of the beholder. In a successful relationship, both parties accept the others' quirks and even find them endearing and funny.

In unsuccessful relationships, those quirks can be what the police call *motive.*

There is an old saying that a man marries a woman hoping she won't change, and a woman marries a man hoping he will. If that's your expectation for a relationship, you're headed for disappointment. People do change, but they don't always change in the ways you want them to. Once you accept people for who they are, you begin to see their quirks' beauty and understand how they add flavor to the relationship.

My golf buddy has a quirk involving planning golf trips down to the most minute detail. He books the flights and hotels, gets the tee times, selects the restaurants, and even researches the history and points of interest of wherever we're going. He's also a bit of a tightwad, so he gets the best deals possible. He genuinely loves to do this because he wants to make sure everything is done to his liking, save money, or control the situation. In any event, I don't care because I hate doing that stuff. I can do it if necessary, but I'm happy to let someone else handle it.

A relationship where both parties accept each other's quirks is liberating. Being who you are, quirks and all is the easiest way to go through life. You don't have to pretend, you don't have to lie, and you don't have to create different versions of yourself depending on the situation. Of course, I recognize that sometimes you might have to tone down some of your quirkier quirks, but in those most cherished relationships, you never have to put your quirks under a blanket.

Robert Fulghum wrote, "We're all a little weird, and life's a little weird, and when we find someone whose weirdness is compatible with ours, we join up with them and fall in mutual weirdness — and call it love – true love."

Think about all your relationships, past and present. How did you first meet each person? Except for blood relatives, you first met the people in your life by happenstance. Maybe you were in the same class or another activity at school. Perhaps you met at a party or restaurant, shared a common interest, worked for the same company, or maybe you were just in a particular place at a specific time and bumped into each other. Happenstance, luck, chance, kismet, or the general randomness of life play a more significant part in our relationships than we admit. We usually don't set about making friends; it just happens. Romantic relationships are much the same. We typically meet our first love in high school or college. Why? Because the biological timing is right, and it's a target-rich environment. As we age, shared interests play a more significant role in our relationships. Regardless of how we meet, some relationships last, and some don't. It's just the nature of the beast. Circumstances change that cause some people to drift out of our lives. Sometimes, one person changes, and the things that brought us close aren't so relevant anymore. If you're a parent, you want to ensure your children associate with friends who will enhance their lives and help keep them safe. You cringe when you hear about a child or young adult who got into trouble because they "hung out with the wrong crowd." As an adult, the same applies.

YOU WANT TO ASSOCIATE YOURSELF WITH PEOPLE WHO ADD TO YOUR HAPPINESS, ENERGIZE YOU, AND MAKE YOU SMILE. PEOPLE WHO MAKE YOU FEEL GOOD JUST BEING AROUND THEM. THESE PEOPLE WILL BE YOUR TRAVELING COMPANIONS ON YOUR JOURNEY TO FIND YOUR EASY WAY TO ENJOY LIFE.

Once I learned that living a lie isn't living, I realized that some people will like me no matter what I do, and others won't. That would have bothered me when I was trying to be all things to all people, but not now. People throw off a vibe, sometimes good and sometimes not so good. I'm sure you've met someone who just rubs you the wrong way, but you don't know exactly why.

On the other hand, you've also met someone you immediately liked but don't know why. It could be their smile, body language, pheromones, voice, or almost anything else. Your friends know your quirks and love you anyway. These people will make every day memorable and who you can count on when you need backup. You might not see a friend for years, but when you get together, it's like you were never apart.

Embrace your quirks and the people who love you despite or because of them, and embrace their quirks, too.

CHAPTER SEVEN

IT'S NOT ALL ABOUT THE BENJAMINS

The economy in the US is based on a straightforward formula. Some people make stuff or provide services, and others buy that stuff or those services. Most of the workforce comprises people employed by the businesses that make the stuff or deliver the services. These workers are paid and use that money to buy the stuff or services their business or other businesses offer. Because of this simple formula, companies spend billions of dollars trying to get us to buy as much of their stuff and services as possible. One way they do that is to suggest that to be envied or admired by others, to feel good about yourself, or to be happy, you must buy their stuff and display it conspicuously. This is a trap, and I confess I've fallen into it more than once. As I've said, I'm a car guy, and I've spent more money than I've needed to on vehicles to get me from point A to point B. Admit it, you've fallen into the trap as well. It's one thing to fall into the trap and quite another to fall so deep that you can't get out.

If you want to find your easy-to-enjoy life, it will be hard without at least some money. The dollar figure will differ for each of us, but it won't be zero. There are lots of ways to acquire money, such as:

You can earn it through your work: Like the old song says, "Get a Job."

You can inherit it: Assuming you won the lucky sperm award.

You can marry it: You can marry more money in a minute than you can earn in a lifetime.

You can steal it: You'll look very fashionable in an orange jump suit.

Someone can give it to you as a gift: I wouldn't count on that happening too often.

You can go treasure hunting and find it: X marks the spot.

You can go to a casino and win it: Because you're smarter and luckier than the owners of those billion-dollar casinos.

And my personal favorite: You can win the lottery: Never mind the 302 million-to-1 odds.

Why is winning the lottery my personal favorite? It's because a 2019 survey by STASH, a consumer investing app, found that more than two-thirds of Millennials consider winning the lottery to be a central feature of their retirement strategy. The survey also found that, for many Americans, winning the lottery is the only plan they have for retirement. About 66% of Millennial men and 58% of Millennial women believe winning the lottery is a reasonable retirement plan. However, they say they would invest it all if they did win the lottery.

You're not going to win the lottery; if you do win it, you'll probably blow it all and be broke within a few years. It happens all the time. It's nice to fantasize about, but so are many other things with a very low probability of occurring.

Let's put money into perspective. If you woke up tomorrow morning and found $1 million in cash at the foot of your bed, you'd be pretty happy, right? What would you say if someone told you they'd give you $1 million right now, but you wouldn't wake up tomorrow morning? You'd turn that person down cold. So, just waking up tomorrow morning is worth more than $1 million. Why? Because if you wake up in the morning, there is still a world of possibilities in front of you. You get to experience love, excitement, humor, discouragement, frustration, and the wide range of emotions all of us feel. You get to visit with friends and family, enjoy your hobbies or outside interests, take on challenges, succeed some, and fail some. You get to live!

You still need enough money to live on, however. Let's assume that none of the options for obtaining money are realistic for you except the one about working for it. That means having a job. Having a job can mean different things. You can start your own business, which requires having a great idea for a product or service, turning that idea into something people want to buy, building some structure that allows you to get that product or service into the marketplace, pricing it so that you can make a profit, selling it, collecting from your customers or clients, paying your employees (even if it's just you), paying your expenses, paying taxes, fighting off the competition, and marketing day and night.

This will take some time and involve quite a bit of risk, but if that's where your passion lies, by all means, go for it.

I started my consulting business in 1982. Here's why I did. My first job out of grad school was teaching psychology at Oklahoma City University (OCU). After being there one year, the dean of the College of

Arts and Sciences decided it would be a great idea if I were promoted to chairman of the psych department. The only earthly reason I can think of for him making me chairman of the department was that the sitting chairman, who hired me, was such a jerk that none of the other faculty wanted to work with him. He had tenure and couldn't be fired, so the dean did the next best thing: demoted him. When my previous boss found out he now worked for me, he showered me with some colorful language that I won't repeat here. At that point, I understood the dean's decision. The only advantage of being chairman of a department at a university is that you get to make out everyone's teaching schedule, so naturally, I gave myself the prime teaching times. I gave the dog times to my former boss. I'm not particularly proud of this, but I'm not too ashamed of it, either. I was young and hadn't learned that vindictiveness isn't a great way to handle conflict. I like to think I'd handle that situation differently now. The biggest takeaway from my chairmanship is that I realized I don't like being a boss.

I left OCU in 1979 to join the psychological consulting firm RHR International. They opened an office in Memphis, so we moved there in 1980. While at RHR, I learned how to consult with businesses and fell in love with consulting. As the third person in a three-person office, I was given the least glamorous assignments, which was fair because I was learning.

I spent much time on the road and missed valuable family time. I'm grateful for my experience with RHR because it gave me the tools to take the next step. My time with RHR made me realize that I don't like being an employee.

Since I knew I didn't like being a boss or an employee, I figured my career options had narrowed down to working for myself. Fortunately, I began working with a client in Nashville and developed a close working relationship with him. His name was Bill Cochran and he was the general agent for Northwestern Mutual, covering central and eastern Tennessee and northern Alabama. He liked what I did for him, assessing candidates to become life insurance salespeople (later called financial advisors) and coaching him and his leadership team. What he didn't like was paying the steep fees that RHR charged. After working with him and his leadership team for a few months, he asked me if I was interested in moving to Nashville and setting up my own consulting business. I hadn't thought about that at the time, but when he put it out there, it struck a chord immediately. We hashed out the details and shook hands on the deal. We moved to Nashville in June 1982, and I've never regretted the move. Mr. Cochran was on the board of one of the big banks in Nashville when they were still locally owned, and he told me he'd introduce me to some of the business leaders in town. He did, and my practice took off. I still call him Mr. Cochran because I greatly respect him; he changed my life. He passed away a few years ago, and I wept openly at his funeral.

I realize this kind of opportunity doesn't come along every day or to every person. For most people, getting and keeping a job is the easiest way to obtain the necessary cash to live on. It's up to you to decide what kind of life you want to live and how much money it will take to live that life. That means coming up with a budget. If you don't have a written budget, I encourage you to do that immediately. It will let you know what expenses are necessary and recurring, like housing, food, clothing, transportation, and utilities, which are occasional and discretionary, like entertainment, travel, and hobbies, and which are just buying stuff because you want to have it. One of the easiest ways to enjoy life is to get out of debt and stay out. I'm no financial wizard, so I can't tell you exactly how to do it, but do it.

I know how and why businesses hire people, what they expect from their employees, and what their employees expect from them. On a broad scale, companies hire a person for three reasons.

First, the business believes that person can help them make money. *Second,* they think that person can help the company save money. *Third,* they believe that person can support the people who make or save the business money.

They definitely don't hire a person because that person needs a job. It's up to the person to demonstrate value to the business. It's also up to the business to show value to the person.

People want a work environment that provides stability, security, acceptance, opportunities to learn and grow, open communication, inspiring leadership, and a place where they can have some fun during the eight or more hours a day they spend there. How much you are paid for your work depends on how much the business and businesses like it believe that work is worth.

How you feel about your compensation can be tricky. Here's a little thought experiment to illustrate the point. Suppose you work for a company that you enjoy working for. You like the people you work with, you like where the company is located, you like your actual job, you are being paid $20/hour, and you believe you are being paid fairly for your work. At this point, you're a happy camper regarding your job.

Then you find out that a coworker in a different office in the same city makes $40/hour for the same job. Are you still happy? I'm guessing not.

Your boss finds out you're unhappy and offers you $30/hour. That's a 50% raise right on the spot. Are you happy now? I'm guessing still not. Your boss then offers you $40/hour, a 100% raise. Are you happy now? Some of you might say you're happier or at least less unhappy, but others might say, "If I'm worth $40/hour now, why wasn't I worth $40/hour last week?"

What you are feeling in that situation is called *relative deprivation.* We might be happy with what we have until we compare ourselves to others who have more of what we desire. You see this in sports all the time. An NFL receiver, let's call him Bob, signs a contract for $10 million a year. He's thrilled. The following year, a receiver on a different team, let's call him Jim, signs a contract for $12 million a year. Bob then complains to anyone who will listen that he feels disrespected because he's only making $10 million. Jim is getting $12 million when Jim's statistics from the previous year weren't as good as Bob's. Remember, Bob signed the contract and was thrilled at the time.

Comparing yourself to others is a game you cannot win.

There will always be those who have more money and stuff. However, money and stuff don't make you happy. Money and stuff do a much better job of making you unhappy than they do of making you happy. If they did make you happy, there wouldn't be so many psychiatrists in Beverly Hills. I think people who are rich and miserable are more miserable than poor and miserable people because everyone is asking them what they have to be miserable about.

Please understand that I'm not talking about serious mental health issues, which cross all socioeconomic lines and are a critical problem in the US. I'm talking about the general discontent and inability to find the joy that some rich and famous seem to experience. The only problems money solves are money problems.

Here's another way that money can be tricky. Take LeBron James, one of the, if not the best, basketball players of all time. I'm betting that when LeBron was a little boy, he loved playing basketball. He probably played all the time, amazing his friends with his abilities. Just the act of playing basketball filled him with joy. He took his talents to the NBA when he graduated from high school. Once in the NBA, he continued to amaze everyone with his abilities and made a lot of money. Let's say that the Lakers owner told LeBron, "LeBron, I appreciate what you've done for us. You're a fantastic basketball player, representing the Lakers and the NBA like few others. Here's the deal. We'd love for you to continue playing for the Lakers, but we're not going to pay you to do so from now on." What's LeBron going to say to that? Probably some variation of "Hell, no." LeBron still loves the game like he did when he was a kid and was playing for the sheer joy of it. However, now he'll only play if he's being paid to do so.

Here's a sad fact of life. External motivation (money, prestige, power, etc.) destroys internal motivation to do something for the joy of doing it or to see how good you can get at it.

To make enough money to meet your basic needs, you most likely need a job if you don't already have one. The market determines how much you can earn from any given position within a range. If you have a job and believe you're underpaid (who doesn't?), it's because economic forces have determined the pay scale for your job. If you have a government job, your pay will be capped because it comes from taxpayers. Whatever a government gives to one person must be taken from someone else. Governments do not create jobs; they make it easier or more difficult for businesses to create jobs. If you have a career in the private sector, there are a few ways to make more money. The *first* is to get good at your job. The top 5% in almost every job do well financially. This could take a lot of time and effort, and you must decide whether it's worth it. The *second* way is to work your ass off, including long hours and time away from family and friends. This is how many entrepreneurs and solopreneurs hit it big when their businesses take off. Again, you need to decide how much effort you're willing to put in.

"Never get so busy making a living that you forget to make a life."

~ Dolly Parton

The Arnold Zack saying, "Nobody on his deathbed ever said, 'I wish I had spent more time on my business'" rings true. A *third* way is to find a job within your company that needs to be done, but everyone hates doing it. I assure you that if you're willing to do that job and do it well, you'll be valued in that company and will survive if there's a business downturn. *Fourth,* you can quit your job and find a job in an industry that pays more. This can be risky if your skill set isn't easily transferrable. *Fifth,* learn how to sell. Salespeople are always in demand and are the engine that drives businesses forward. Selling looks easy to some, but it's not. If it were, everyone would do it. Salespeople are well-paid, especially commission salespeople because they create and maintain customers or clients.

To survive in commission sales, you must be prepared for income variability. I learned this when I started my consulting business. Big projects were followed by sparse activity. At times, I didn't know whether I was rich or poor. It evened out over time, but when you're self-employed and provide a service, you wake up every morning without a job and must create one.

OK, you've got a job that pays you enough to enjoy your life. Parkinson's law states that expenditures rise to meet income. Restated, the more you make, the more you spend. Economists call this lifestyle creep. If you want to continue to enjoy your life from a money standpoint, you must break that cycle. How do you do that?

Pay yourself first! It's that simple.

Change your mindset so that you think of your long-term financial health as a bill that you must pay every month and pay it before you pay all your other bills. That means you can't buy all the cool stuff you'd like to until you've paid yourself. *The second key is to quit buying shit you don't need.* I know the thrill of seeing Amazon packages arrive at your doorstep can be intoxicating, but do you really need an air fryer? *A third key is to stop trying to keep up with the Joneses.* For all you know, the Joneses are trying to keep up with you. All you see from the Joneses is what they want you to see. You don't know what's going on behind closed doors. If you keep your financial house in order and ignore the Joneses, you might look out your window one day and see a FOR SALE sign on their front lawn because they got overextended.

Money is a sensitive subject for many people. It's a significant contributor to divorces. It's also a significant contributor to marriages. There are few things people care about more than their money. H. L. Mencken said, "When somebody says it's not about the money, it's about the money." Whenever you enter into a relationship where money could become an issue, it's a good idea to have the "money talk" early on.

People in business have a much easier time having the money talk than people in personal relationships. They outline the parameters of the relationship: who owns what, who gets paid what, who must pay what, and so on. Then, they sign a contract with all those particulars spelled out. All financial dealings are a contract of one kind or another.

My oldest son was an excellent tennis player. He played all the time and, as a result, broke many strings on his racket. I was playing a lot of tennis then and breaking strings as well. At first, I had the pro at the tennis club string our rackets. Then I got my bill from the club and realized that each stringing cost about $20, even though the strings only cost about $5. I brought this to my son's attention (he was around 14 at the time) and asked if he had any ideas about how to cut the cost of stringing rackets. He had no suggestions other than having Dad continue to pay, but I had an idea.

I told him I would buy him a racket stringing machine, and he would learn to string his rackets. Furthermore, I told him he could string rackets for others and charge them whatever he thought his time was worth. I encouraged him to do that because he would have to pay me back for the stringing machine somehow, but once he did, everything he earned stringing rackets was pure profit going into his pocket.

My son was and is a bright person and saw the wisdom in my suggestion, since the other option was to try to play tennis with no strings in his racket. He paid me back quickly and made about $2,000 that summer. I was proud of him, and he was proud of himself. The money you earn feels much better in your pocket than the money given to you.

Here's an idea if you're entering a romantic relationship that you think might lead to something long-term. Run a credit check on your romantic interest. I know this sounds cold, but when you marry someone, you marry their debts and assets. "Love will keep us together" is bullshit, and you know it. People who have successful relationships have tremendous teamwork when it comes to money. They have a budget, know who's responsible for what, don't keep secrets about money from one another or lie about it, and they're concerned about themselves as a couple and no one else. Money doesn't become a barrier to their easy way to enjoy life.

There is a direct relationship between how much money you have and the choices you can make. More money leads to more choices. However, that doesn't mean that if you have money, you'll make good choices. In fact, money expands the range of bad choices you can make. You can begin to feel untouchable, and that feeling somehow turns off the commonsense areas of your brain.

Rarely does a day go by that you don't see, hear, or read about a public figure in politics, entertainment, or sports who has managed to do something incredibly stupid. Probably the most common is getting a DUI. When I see this, I shake my head in amazement. How hard is it to get an Uber? If you've got that much money, hire a limo and let someone drive you around to wherever so you can do whatever for as long as you please.

Recently, an NBA player lost a potential $37 million by getting suspended for brandishing a gun in public, not once but twice. If you want to play with guns, there are shooting ranges everywhere. Public intoxication and violence toward others aren't the exclusive domain of the rich and famous, but the repercussions can be magnified. I guess the moral of this story is that just because you can do it, it doesn't mean you should do it.

One more thing. Once you achieve financial security, go ahead and spend some of it on the things that give you joy, especially experiences. Nobody is guaranteed tomorrow. The Malcolm Forbes quote, "He who dies with the most toys, wins," is bullshit.

"After the game, the king and the pawn go into the same box."

~ Italian Proverb

Good judgment costs nothing but yields tremendous rewards. The more thoughtful you are about money, the easier it will be for you to NJOYLFE.

AUTHOR NOTES AND CLOSING THOUGHTS

The idea for this book has been percolating in my brain for several years. I even wrote down a title in 2015 (not the one for this book) and saved it to my file labeled "Book to write someday." I observe people for a living, and I started noticing that many people seemed to lack the capacity to enjoy life.

I saw anger, anxiety, envy, jealousy, divisiveness, depression, confusion, resentment, disrespect, lawlessness, and broad discontent coming to the forefront of daily life, at least according to social and other media.

At the same time, I saw others who seemed to be having the time of their lives. I wondered what the difference between the groups was. I could have done a rigorous study using the scientific method to find the statistical differences between the groups, but I decided against it. Why? Because it's too damned hard, and I'm all about finding my easy way to NJOYLFE.

I started a different book in May 2022, but the idea for this book kept popping into my head, and it distracted me to the point where I figured I'd either write it or quit thinking about it.

I've shared several personal stories because I want you, dear reader, to get a sense of who I am and why I'm so passionate about helping people find joy. I hope that I've been able to unlock the joy in you that's either been missing or overwhelmed by the avalanche of negativity that bombards us every day.

Thank you for reading my book. I have a small favor to ask. If you have suggestions for improvements, please email me at <u>angelo@angelovalenti.com</u> and let me know what I can do better. I love feedback, positive or negative.

If you liked what you read, especially if it made a positive difference in your life, *please leave an honest review on Amazon.* Reviews are the best way for others to purchase the book and find their easy way to NJOYLFE.

I am honored that you chose to spend this time with me, and I hope it has been a helpful experience.

Now, go out and discover *YOUR* easy way to NJOYLFE!

LET'S WORK TOGETHER

I've enjoyed working with businesses and individuals for over 40 years, and I'm still as excited as the day I opened my practice. I've reached an age where if it's been a while since I've seen someone, the first question they ask is, "Are you still working?" My answer is always, "My retirement party and my funeral are going to be on the same day."

If you are:

- A businessperson who wants to build your team by hiring the right people for your company's unique culture and develop the talent in your organization,

- A leader or potential leader who wants to sharpen your leadership skills and work on becoming the best version of yourself,

- Looking for a speaker with an uplifting (and funny) message for your next meeting,

- Ready to find YOUR personal easy way to NJOYLFE.

Let's visit!

You can book a discovery call by going
to ReachAngelo.com

My consulting website is
www.thecompanypsychologist.com, and my email
is valenti@thecompanypsychologist.com

You can find me on Facebook @Angelo Valenti or
Instagram @companypsychdoctor

Please message me on LinkedIn:
https://www.linkedin.com/in/angelovalentiphd/

Please send me an email at:
angelo@angelovalenti.com

Visit my publishing website:
angelovalenti.com

I'd love to hear your story and help you write the
next chapters.

ABOUT THE AUTHOR

Dr. Angelo Valenti grew up in Cleveland (Shaker Heights, to be exact). Still, he had the good sense to move away after graduating from Case Western Reserve University with a degree in psychology (sorry, Cleveland, but you know, it's Cleveland). He played football and baseball in high school and college and continues his athletic pursuits on the golf course.

He earned an MS and Ph.D. in social psychology from the University of Georgia and is a card-carrying member of the American Psychological Association (APA) and the APA Division of Consulting Psychology. He is also the co-author of the 2005 game-changer *Unleashing Leadership: Aligning What Your People Do Best With What Your Organization Needs Most.*

Dr. Valenti is a psychologist, consultant, and professional coach with more than four decades of experience helping individuals and organizations understand how to reach goals, break free of constraints, and be the best version of themselves for personal and professional success. His experience includes teaching psychology at Oklahoma City University and serving as a consultant with RHR International before starting his practice.

He assesses talent for various industries and is passionate about helping companies find the right individuals to fit their unique cultures. He firmly believes that "Companies hire for skills but fire for attitude." He coaches leaders and those who want to be leaders, increasing their effectiveness as leaders and becoming the best versions of themselves. He says, "People are capable of dramatic change and growth. Sometimes, they need a guide to help them figure out what to change, how to change, and why that change will be of value to them." Dr. Valenti also coaches people who want to find their personal easy way to NJOYLFE.

Based in Nashville, TN, he runs his private consulting practice and serves as the go-to expert for companies across a variety of industries, including:

- Retail
- Healthcare
- Publishing
- Financial Services
- Distribution
- Insurance
- Telecommunications
- Security
- Transportation Services

But Dr. Valenti's true "joy" comes largely from his amazing wife, his three wonderful children, and five grandchildren.

GRATITUDE

Just as life is a journey, writing this book has been a journey, and without the support and guidance of my team, I would surely have gotten lost in the weeds. (If you knew how bad my sense of direction is, you'd know I get lost a lot).

Thanks to my wonderful wife, Rachel, my soulmate, who somehow finds my quirks endearing, always speaks the truth and makes it easy to enjoy life.

Thanks to my three sons, Matt, Joey, and Dylan, for being a constant source of joy, an occasional source of agita, and my only source of grandchildren.

Thanks to the clients I've worked with over the last 40-plus years. I've learned so much from you, and I hope you've also learned a little from me.

Thanks to my writing coach, Honoree Corder, who showed me the WHAT, HOW, and WHY of writing a book and did so in an inspiring and entertaining way.

Thanks to my editor, Karen Hunsanger, my cover designer and formatter, Dino Marino, and my copy editor and proofreader, Nick Georgandis, for their skill and patience.

www.ingramcontent.com/pod-product-compliance
Lightning Source LLC
Chambersburg PA
CBHW050549160726
48003CB00002B/822